Facebook Marketing

The Definitive Beginner's Guide

Leverage Facebook, Maximize Your Exposure And Reach Tons Of Potential Customers On A Shoestring Budget

By Adam Richards

\

Table of Contents

Introduction

Facebook is perhaps one of the most powerful sites in today's times. You can find innumerable people logging in to their accounts daily to catch a glimpse of what's buzzing on the internet, what is up with the lives of their friends and so much more.

However, the topic which pertain to our interests the most has to be how Facebook marketing has become one of the top tools for those who have a business bent of mind. It is extremely important to tap the huge growth which Facebook marketing has to offer.

In this book, I am going to take you through some of the different ways by which you can make the most out of your need to leverage the most out of Facebook marketing.

The kind of reach which Facebook can offer is whopping and this is why you should be willing to explore the different aspects of how you can enjoy the most out of Facebook.

Facebook has immense potential and it can connect you to too many people. The kind of strategies which you are using when you are working on Facebook marketing assumes pivotal importance. When you check out the different details I have listed in this book, you will be much more equipped to get a clear idea of how the whole thing operates.

Facebook marketing is one of the most effective marketing forms and you should ideally put in ample efforts to ensure that you can maximize the overall reach which you can obtain from your Facebook campaign.

Even if you are a complete novice and you have no prior detail of how to engage in Facebook marketing, I am here to assist you. Some people wonder of the amount of money that will be incurred as expenses. You need to know that there are various free schemes as well which you can choose. When you pick these free methods, this is going to simplify the troubles for you.

So, let us get started in our endeavor to help you learn a budget way of making the most out of Facebook marketing. Before you proceed with this book, I will recommend you to use this book not just for the sake of reading it, but you need to follow the points as well. Every point which I will talk about in this book needs to be understood and then implemented. This is the only way by which you will be able to reap the maximum output from it.

Chapter 1:

Getting You To A Quick Start

Now that you have decided to make the most out of Facebook marketing, here is the time to get to a quick start. In this chapter, I will simply acquaint you with the main points to give you an idea of what you are getting into.

We will be dealing with the details in the subsequent chapter. However, this chapter is going to give you the right head start which can turn out to be handy when you are looking to explore the right avenues in the field of marketing.

Make Your Own Page

The first thing which you need to do is get your business a Facebook page. Opening a page is easy and free of cost. However, just because opening a page is free of cost doesn't infers that you can dive into this topic without a clear discussion of the key things.

When you are listing your Facebook page, there are important considerations you need to make. You have to keep an eye on the name of the page you are using, the keywords you are targeting and the kind of demographics and categories you choose.

Setting up a page is the very first step and it is important that you dig the details earnestly to be sure that you are doing it in an orderly manner. I will guide you with the details of setting a page by picking the finest parameters which will be of help.

Reach Out To People

If you make your own Facebook page and then sit back and do nothing; it is almost like having a shop with no products. What are people going to do with an empty shop which offers no products? Nobody is ever going to come to you. So, you need to come up with the right kind of actions which will help you in reaching out to a lot of people.

There are various strategies and tips which you can follow for the sake of reaching out to your potential customers. This forms the meat of the marketing strategies. When you are trying to reach out to potential customers, you should opt for a blend of both paid and free marketing ways.

I will take you through both the methods and by striking an optimum blend of the two; you will be able to learn some of the most important details that will shape your Facebook marketing campaign in the right manner.

Keep Up The Work

The next thing you need to do is keep the momentum going. If you are not putting in the right work, the efforts which you have put so far might go down the drain.

Remember that Facebook marketing is a dynamic topic and so you should try and keep the momentum going or else the results shall turn out to be miserable. This is why it is important to keep an eye on the periodic updates that can keep coming.

You should always have a look at the dashboard and analyze how many people have been visiting your posts, the countries which show the maximum interest, the percentage of people who interact on your post, the output which the organic search generates and so on.

Thus, putting in the right amount of work is extremely important and you have to keep on working upon your Facebook page.

Now that you have some idea of how Facebook marketing needs to be carried out, let us get to the core details and explore the different points thoroughly.

When you are working on your marketing plan, you have to put in your best efforts and make sure not to back out from the things you wish to achieve.

Chapter 2:

Facebook Pages – Kick Start Your Marketing Campaign

This is the first and foremost step which you need to bear in mind. Make sure to follow the different points listed here and then you will be all set to make the most out of your Facebook marketing campaign.

There are more than 50 million pages that currently exist on Facebook and when it comes to Facebook users, the count is more than 829 million people which means that the kind of access which you can get is tremendously whopping.

Further, you need to know that people who use Facebook span different kind of age groups. As per statistical reports, 31% of the total Facebook users fall in the age group of 35 – 54 which is mostly the cream of the target customers for nearly all kinds of business.

However, there are other age groups too who are pretty popular on Facebook. So, you should make it a point to set up a Facebook page because a larger part of your target customers are already present there. With the right kind of fine tuning, you will be able to reap the right kind of dividends which in turn can boost your business in ways more than one.

Now that you are aware of the demographics, we will start with the process of setting up a page. Let us get down to the main steps.

Pick An Apt Classification

When you are setting up a Facebook page, you will find different kinds of classifications which you can pick from. Setting up a page is not something you should do without thorough discussion. The page you are setting up needs to fall under a category and this is why you should check out the different categories, analyze which one seems to best depict what you are looking for and then choose the same.

The six different categories which you will find when opening a Facebook page are as follows.

Local business or place: it is used for companies that are looking to target the local demographics.

Company, organization or institution: all companies can use this category for the sake of building their brand and promoting it earnestly.

Brand or product: this category is meant specifically for products and not for brands as a

whole.

\# Entertainment: this is ideally for those who are looking to get new releases and talk about upcoming ventures.

\# Artist, band or public figure: this is targeted for individuals who want to promote their own work.

\# Cause or community: this is mainly for charitable causes which needs a community to come forward and pledge their support.

When you are picking a category, you should carefully check out these categories and then pick the one which seems closest to what you are looking for in your business. Be careful about what you pick because you will have to fill in a few particulars that shall pertain to your page.

Choosing a random category shall not serve any use because you will not be able to fine tune your targeted customers. This is why I would advise you to visit pages of your competitors and study them to draw some points. Unless you are completely familiar with what you want from your business, it is best advised to visit similar pages and draw the much needed details.

Fill In The Particulars

The next thing which you need to do is fill in the particulars for your company. While Facebook pages do not call for a great deal of information, but you are requested to put in as much as it is feasible for you. Ideally, the page should be listed in a way that it looks credible and people can actually rely on it and get something constructive out of it.

When you are adding the information, it is always requested from you to put up a profile picture. Remember, you need to be careful when you do so because the profile picture is the image which you are projecting. So, do not put up anything randomly. Both the profile as well as the cover picture should be such that it ends up representing your page in an apt manner. The company logo seems to work best.

You should pin the business page as a favorite as this will bookmark your page in your newsfeed section. When you do all this set up, you will be prompted to create an ad for the sake of starting up. Our advice to you is not to put in money for the advertisement instantly after setting up your page. The reason is that people hardly know about your page and they are least likely to be interested in the same.

Work As An Admin

With a new page comes new responsibility. You are now the administrator of your page and so you need to be familiar with the admin duties and responsibilities.

It may take some time to get familiar with the admin view of your page and you need to invest time for the same. You will find different types of metrics on the right hand side including the total likes in a week, the messages you have received, the notification count and so on. All these data hold significant importance and you should pay heed to them for the sake of leveraging the most out of your page.

You will also find a settings option in the left hand panel and clicking on that will open up a wide range of different options for you. You will find options for configuring the different details. You can add in more details about your page in the page info section. Further, you can regulate the amount of notification you receive by setting up page alert as well.

You also find an option called page roles wherein you can add more people to the pages. Doing this will help you distribute the work. One of the best things about administering the roles is that there are different designations which mean that you can offer restricted power to different people and thereby develop your page much more efficiently.

So, you must spend time exploring the different options which you have. The more you explore, the better you will be able to get an idea of how things work and thus your page will benefit the most from it.

Time For Content Building

The next step which you need to perform is to be sure that you put in the right content. You have to work upon building the content as it is going to give you the right direction. When people visit your page, it is the content that will force them to stay there. If your page has no content, how do you expect to build up on it?

There are umpteen strategies which you can choose for the sake of content building. In the subsequent chapters, we are going to discuss the details of the paid and free methods which you can choose for popularizing the content and even posting it in an apt manner.

One common mistake which a lot of business pages do is that they end up posting the content in clusters. You will find a lot of pages that have too much content on a single day and then long gaps for consecutive days.

This is not the best strategy and can turn out to be wrong for a lot of reasons.

This is why you should make it a point to schedule your posts such that the posts can be spread uniformly all throughout the day. Apart from this, you also need to keep an eye on the call to actions.

If your page is geared with a business point of view, you need to have some clickable action links. What use are the posts going to be, if people have no clue where to go? This is why you need to think thoroughly before posting content on your Facebook page.

Do not post content merely to populate your page because having unrelated content is not going to work. There are two mean reasons as to why you should post content.

Firstly, to gather the right audience for your post and secondly, you should do it for the sake of offering the right content to your followers. When they come to your page, they should feel like the content they are going through offers them some kind of value. So, keeping both these points in mind, you should then work upon the different posts and then populate your page in the desired manner such that traffic can peak.

Once there is ample content, you can then ask your prospective customers to like the page. This stage is extremely extensive and can entail plenty of time and effort. You should once again opt for both paid and free methods of working as it will give you the right exposure which in turn is going to help you in clinching your business objective.

Analyze The Activity Tab

Once you have put in ample content and you also have quite a lot of people liking the posts, the next thing you need to do is concentrate upon the activity page. There are a lot of different details which you will find under the activity head.

It is important to keep an eye on the activity tab because this will show you the kind of engagement you are going to get on your site. Once you are familiar with the same, you can then work upon the right strategies which will turn out to be of help.

This is an overview of the different aspects which will help you in being sure that you are carrying out Facebook marketing strategies in an apt manner.

Now, you have ample information to get started. I will offer you more details with factual aspects that will guide you into understanding how to extract the most out of Facebook marketing on a budget.

Chapter 3:

Operating Your Facebook Page The Right Way

The art of setting a Facebook page is already known to you as we have discussed the core aspects already in the previous chapter. However, when we are setting a page, there is more to it than merely making the setup.

As you already know of the need to populate your page with ample content, the million dollar question remains as to what type of content you should post, the frequency of posting, the need to host giveaways and contests and more.

This chapter will help you get familiar with all these points and you are going to learn some of the most important points related to the same.

Curate The Right Content

The first thing you need to keep in mind is the need to curate the perfect content. When you are working on your Facebook page, you will have to keep on posting the content periodically.

However, you cannot post just about anything. So, here are some tips which will help you in understanding as to what would be the best content posting strategies.

Research about what the target customers need

You should find out what people are actually looking for. It is important to put in the right kind of research wherein you get an idea of the content which falls in the theme of your business and at the same time can interest the followers as well. The more you research, the more details you will get and this will help you in improving your page content.

Post interesting content

The content which you post should ideally be such that it interests people. Having too much of boring content that isn't really useful is not going to be of help. So, you should make it a point to find out the type of content which is most likely to interest the followers.

If you share interesting content, it will help you engage your followers and this in turn is going to help you gain more followers. The reaction which is set off can be a chain reaction and thus you are sure to improve your page insights much more substantially.

Time your posts

You have to be sure that you are posting the content periodically. If you are going to post too much content together and then intersperse it with too much gaps, it is going to be termed as bad marketing strategy. There are plenty of different solutions which you can use. Some of them come at a premium and they offer you plenty of features as you can post the same update on multiple media channels at once. Argyle social, HootSuite, buffer, sprout social are some of the apps that are often used. You will find that too many of them come at a hefty price. Based upon your budget, you need to filter the different options so that you can come up with the ideal choice you could possibly opt for.

Hold contests and giveaways

This is another important point you need to bear in mind. You should make it a point to hold multiple contests and giveaways. When you are holding contests, you need to ensure that you are trying to get ample reach. If your contests do not attract plenty of people, the whole use of hosting it in the first place is going to fail.

So, there is a lot of thought that you should put in prior to holding contests. When you are keeping an eye on the details, it will be easier for you to come up with the right kind of schemes that can be of help.

When you are organizing giveaways, you should list the complete details and then try and offer plenty of incentives which will help the followers in taking part in these contests. You do not need to have too many contests together but the idea is to try and have contests at regular intervals such that you can bring in good amount of engagement.

Whenever you have a contest, you should work upon the main prize which you need to offer. When you have an excellent prize to offer, it will get people interested and thus it is going to make your promotional campaigns successful. I will help you with more details in the field of organizing contests in the subsequent chapter.

The right call to action

The next thing you need to mind when making the perfect post is to incorporate an appropriate call to action. You have to direct your followers to doing something. If you sit back and hope that they are going to do it on their own, your marketing campaign is all set to fail.

So, you should try and choose the best call to action strategies which will actually help you in accomplishing your objective. Try and make it very clear as to what you expect from your followers.

Have a clear action button which the users can choose and thereby benefit from the same. If you do not list it clearly, things are not going to improve for you.

While it is not mandatory that every post needs to have an action call, you should at least try your bit with it. When you offer an action button, you need to list ample reasons to actually convince your followers to do the same. This is the perfect recipe to ensure that your followers actually contribute towards your business goals.

The ultimate motive of your business page is to boost your business and profits and if you can gain a larger exposure, it is one added benefit to the same. So, you should not miss out on the importance of putting up an action button.

These are some of the details that will help you in having the perfect page which can be of help. However, we are now going to talk of some budget methods which will help you in improving the overall engagement on your site. There are plenty of different ways by which you can push the amount of exposure and reach which your Facebook pages get and we are going to deal with the same.

Chapter 4:

Facebook Groups And How To Make The Most Out Of Them

Are you a part of Facebook groups? You must be aware of the different groups that exist on Facebook. There is no dearth of such groups and you can find too many of them easily.

However, what you need to know is that joining just

about any group is not going to serve your need. You have to be sure that you are choosing such groups which will actually be of help and offer something constructive to you or your business.

This is why I am going to guide you into picking the best groups you could possibly choose and the ways by which they can be of help.

What Are Groups All About?

Before you join a Facebook group, you need to first understand what a group is all about. Merely visiting a group and taking a look at few of the posts should give you an idea. Some groups are closed as the activities are only viewable by the members.

In such cases, you can check out a group's overview as it will give you some kind of an idea as to what can you expect from this group.

If you find that a group seems to bear the same theme as what you are looking for, you are free to participate in the decision to join the group. Take your time and choose the groups you should be a part of. As being a part of a group is not going to cost you anything, you can be a little liberal in your choices.

The reason I am asking you to make some research before being a part of a group is because when you pick the right groups, it is going to help you in filtering the choices in the right manner and this will filter unwanted junk which will serve no need.

If you are a part of groups whose target audience is widely different from what you are looking for, it shall absolutely serve no need and you are not likely to interact in that group either.

So, try and gauge some idea before coming to the final decision as to which groups seem to be best for improving your business output.

Participate In Groups

When you are a part of a group, you need to participate in it. Until and unless, you have an active participation in a group, you will not be able to extract the most out of the group. I am not asking you to spam the group with too many posts; asking the group members to like your page and increase the engagement.

However, you need to know as to how you can participate in different groups. Try and interact a little and build your own community. The amount of members that are a part of Facebook group can be whopping. You can find groups with more than 10k+ active members.

In such groups, when you are interacting with the members; the odds of getting larger and higher engagement is going to be much better. When you are looking to build a community, you may have to talk to other people and even improve their business engagement as well.

The world works on 'give and take' principle. You will have to help someone out in order to enjoy the same perks. So, you should make it a point to check out a group, try and visit the profile of the active members and then work upon the different ways by which you can improve the kind of support and friendship you have with them.

When you participate in groups, you will be able to maximize the overall reach which your page can get. Not only this, even when you are holding contests and giveaways, you can share the details of the same in groups.

When you are offering such information in groups, it is best advised to check that your post concurs with the theme of the group. There are various groups where moderators make it a point to list down some specifications and you need to adhere to the same. Failure to abide by the rules can force moderators to remove you from the group.

So, explore the details diligently and then work your way towards ensuring that your group participation can help you in improved Facebook page activities.

Free Of Cost

One of the best benefits which a Facebook group has to offer is that it comes entirely free of cost. You do not need to deal with any unwanted hassles of paying a fee for the sake of participating in these groups. Some groups can also offer you 'like exchange' program. While you should check how legitimate the likes are really going to be, but if you get it free of cost, you can definitely try your luck and be hopeful that in the end, the rewards are going to be in favors of you.

So, when you want to make the most out of Facebook marketing and you have a budget to abide by, I would recommend exploring Facebook groups and then trying out how they can fine tune the success you can achieve.

Chapter 5:

Facebook Advertising Campaigns Explained

When you are looking to make the most out of Facebook marketing, you need to invest in the best advertisement campaigns which you can pick. Here we are going to talk of some of the most diverse and different kinds of advertising campaigns which can be implemented on Facebook.

When you have a Facebook page, you will need plenty of interaction and engagement. While you can list free advertisements, they may not always offer you right value. Facebook has a very strange way of regulating who can view your posts and so too often page owners have to fall back upon paid advertising campaigns.

When you are a part of paid advertisement campaigns, you can regulate the amount of people you will reach, the estimated budget you have, the demographics you can mainly target and so on. Facebook insight offers you plenty of details and thus you will have too much of power.

This means that you can choose the amount of money you wish to invest based upon the needs that you have and the kind of reach you want to attain. Having the parameters at hand ensures that you will be able to spend as much as needed.

The Top 5 Targeting Options

When you use Facebook advertisement campaigns, following are the 5 targeting options which you need to work upon.

Location

This factor helps you in selecting the top location where you want to focus upon. Often people set a Facebook page for targeting local business and intruding in the local market. If you have a similar objective, you should try and fill in the particulars of the cities and areas you want to focus upon. This will ensure that your advertisements will be displayed much more in profiles of people who hail from the mentioned region.

Demographics

There are different demographical details which you can keep your eyes on. There are points like age, education, gender and more. With these points, you can exercise greater control over those whom you want to target. As paid advertisement campaigns can entail pretty high money, people are always looking to optimize the most out of it. This is why you should target the ones who can actually benefit from your business.

Interests

You also have the option of reaching out to people based upon the type of hobbies and interests which they have. Feel free to add in particulars about the hobbies which you are interested in. If you use it in the right manner, it is one of the best ways of actually reaching out to the core segment that will truly benefit your business page.

Behaviors

You can also find out details like device usage, the activities, the purchasing patterns and more. These are more subjective points and by monitoring them, you can also improve the focus you have in your advertisement campaign.

Connections

You can choose to promote your advertisement among a specific group of connection, say to the attendees of a specific event or so. This is especially designed for highly specific group of people. It is suited for those who have an advertisement for a specific niche.

These are some of the options which you have at hand. You are free to explore the details and then you can pick the ones that seem to suit your advertising need in an apt manner.

Remember, this is a very crucial step because when you opt for paid Facebook advertisements, your actual advertising cost depends upon the parameters you are choosing and the amount of boost you want for your post.

In this cost sensitive market, it is critical to keep an eye on the parameters that will influence your marketing output.

Should You Boost Your Posts?

Have you heard of Facebook boosting of posts? If you have ever made a Facebook page, you will find the option of boosting your post. A lot of people wonder as to what it truly is and how is it going to be of help.

The answer is pretty simple. Boosting of post infers pushing the reach of your post and making sure that a larger number of people will be viewing it.

When you choose to boost a post, the advertisements are forcibly displayed on the home feed of different people. This will not only increase the viewership of the post but in most cases it has been found that it ends up increasing the overall likes and engagement on your page as well.

However, boosting a post is not free of cost and you will have to pay Facebook quite a lot of money for the same. Hence, the answer as to whether or not you should choose the option of boost post depends entirely upon the budget you have.

You can choose the budget and get a boost accordingly. Facebook post boost is extremely effective, but you should use it selectively. Save it for important posts that are very crucial for your firm. If you have an extremely big event which you want to be thoroughly successful, make a post about the same and then boost it. This will ensure that the post shall spread much larger and wider than what it would have otherwise received.

So, you need to be a little tactical and smart when you are choosing this option.

Chapter 6:

Making Your Very First Advertisement With Step-By-Step Instructions

Now that you have an idea of the parameters which you can control and how budget influences the different points, I will now help you create your very first advertisement.

Remember, advertisements will help you get more

people to come to your page and this is why the particulars you choose like the budget, the demographics, the targeted countries and more, should all be in tandem with what your business entails.

This is not a field where you can afford to be reckless. The field of social media has huge scope and you need to tap the most out of it.

Here, I will list down the simple steps which you should try to follow. When you follow them in the right manner, it will help you understand the best ways by which you can create the perfect advertisement that shall guide you into improving your business prospects.

Get On The Advertisement Page

Login to your profile and on the right hand corner, under the drop box; you will find an option titled, "create an ad". Once you click on that, you will land up on the page called, "Advertise on Facebook".

Linking Your Advertisements

When you are on the page and you are looking to start the process of making an ad, Facebook will prompt you as to what do you want your advertisement to be linked to.

You can redirect people to your company website, blog or any other specific URL you intend to. Alternately, you can send them to other Facebook pages and groups. The decision is entirely yours and should be taken after careful consideration of your marketing objectives.

The Main Aim Of The Advertisement

The next thing you need to do is state the goal of the advertisement. It is important to tell Facebook as to what are you looking to achieve with the help of the ad. You can choose to get more likes or even promote some specific posts that pertain to your interests and likings.

You can also choose to promote a specific website

with the help of your advertisement. The advanced options tab will allow you to enter details of the website which you wish to promote and then you can leverage your Facebook fans to promote another website which is a part of your business.

Advertisement Designing

Once you have filled in these parameters, the next thing to do is to ensure that you design your ad in an appealing manner. Facebook automates most of the task which means that you can merely regulate a few points and you will be all set to design the rest of the advertisement.

You need to put in a killer headline. The character limit is merely 25 and so you should come up with something catchy and entertaining.

Enter the text in the ad. The text can be 90 characters long which mean that you need to be creative once again and work your way towards ensuring that you can really convince your fans and followers to follow the link and catch the remaining details.

While Facebook can automate this for you, I would still advice you to customize it and write them yourself; keeping in mind your own needs and things that shall suit your business in a diligent manner.

You will also have the option of adding a picture in the advertisement. The resolution of the picture is nearly 100x72 pixels and you should make it a point to upload one of nearly same dimensions. This will ensure better clarity. If you upload a picture with a larger image size, Facebook will automatically resize it for you.

Before you write your ad copy, it is important to read their advertisement policy because Facebook has a long list of rules regarding what you should do and the things you need to refrain from posting. This is why being aware of the details of the Facebook advertising policy will guide you into understanding the right ways by which you can make the most out of your marketing campaign.

Targeting Your Ad

The next thing you need to look forward is the targeting of your ad. When you are ready with the headline and the body, you will find the need to focus upon the advertisement.

Facebook will automatically pull data and show you the amount of intended audience along with the total bid amount as well. When you have both these numbers to play with, you can then adjust either or both of them to come down to your own decision as to which among the two seems to be apt for you.

You will find the option to micro target as well because if you have a very specific ad campaign wherein you are looking to exclusively target the locals, you can put in the pin codes of specific areas and then target the

Facebook users of that area.

Facebook is aware of the need to further control other points. This is why you will find too many other details in the advanced options. Like I told you before, you can put in filters like gender, age, relationship status, languages spoken and more.

With all these parameters, it is going to be a lot easier for you to make your advertisement customized enough to target the segment of users you really want to focus upon.

Such is the specificity of the parameters offered that you can target as less as 20 users and as huge as 167 million users as well.

So, the final choice is going to be yours as you are free to pick whatever it is that you deem fit, based upon your budget and business model as well.

Scheduling And Pricing

The next thing you will have to mind is the complete pricing structure and even scheduling of your advertisement. You should name your campaign as it will help you sort from the different campaigns which you may hold later. I would recommend you to have descriptive names for your campaigns such that it is easier for you to remember which campaign was targeted for what objective.

The next thing you need to do is make sure that you set up the right budget. When you are working upon your Facebook advertisement, the amount of money which you are willing to invest is a very important factor.

While I would not suggest you to shoot well beyond your budget, but you are requested to take into account the amount of benefits which the advertisements have the potential to generate. So, make your calculations thoroughly and then come to the right point regarding how much money you think is the right budget.

Once you have settled with your overall budget, the next thing you need to finalize is whether you want to set up a daily budget or you are looking to spend a lump-some amount. Based upon whatever seems best for you, you can choose either of the options.

There are other options too as you can choose to pay per click or you can even agree to pay for every thousand impressions as well. These are the tiny details which you should closely analyze and decide after weighing out monetary decisions and planning.

After filling in all these details, you can proceed and make the payment. You will have plenty of options as you can choose from credit card, PayPal, direct debit and even Facebook ad coupon, if you have one.

Monitoring Your Campaign

The next step is to monitor what the campaign is doing for you. Keep an eye on the different points and try and analyze the ways by which you can actually monitor the kind of progress you are making.

You will find a tab called ads manager and using it will help you find greater insights into your campaign. Click on the campaign name which you intend to monitor and soon you will find a detailed snapshot in front of you.

You will be able to access plenty of details including the number of people who have viewed your ad, the number of click which your ad has generated and even the click through as well. You can also get details like how often the advertisement pops up in the newsfeed. Make sure to closely study the details and then re-work upon your ad in the way you deem fit.

You can always consult your marketing personnel to get some kind of idea as to what seems to be the ideal way to work around your advertisement. You can also generate a complete ad report as this report will have all factual data and statistics under one single document.

This document can be forwarded to your marketing team who can then analyze, improvise and work upon the different parameters to ensure that you come up with the right business decision.

These are the top steps which, if implemented in an orderly manner can take your Facebook marketing campaign to place.

No doubt, you will have to check out other strategies as well which will help in growing your email list. You can always fall back on Facebook for the sake of making a good and commendable email list.

Try and check out as many options as you possibly have because it is sure to guide you in the right direction. Every single stage of the advertisement process is important right from the scratch till the very end.

Look at the endless ways using which you can promote your business and get the most out of it. There is immense scope in online marketing and when you make the most out of social networking sites, you will be able to push your business to new heights.

When you are making a marketing campaign, the email list which you have assumes gargantuan importance. When you have an active Facebook profile or even when your page has a very high engagement, you will be able to build a strong email list.

With a huge email list, you can be hopeful that your marketing campaign is going to spread far and huge and this in turn will assist you in making the most out of your ad campaigns.

Conclusion

Now that you are aware of the different details and strategies which can be used for the sake of Facebook marketing, you should be all set to implement it.

We have discussed ways and methods which will fall in your budget. As Facebook advertisements offer you the provision of setting the budget, it is entirely upon you to finalize the detail of the amount of money you are willing to spend on marketing expenses.

So, feel free to work upon the different details and implement them. When you are keeping an eye on the insights, it is going to help you immensely in shaping your marketing campaign in an apt manner.

Now, when you have the right knowledge and expertise in this area, you will have to implement the details. Feel free to go through the book as many times as needed because the details listed here are practical tips that are sure to guide you in an apt manner.

Facebook has become one of the most important places for the sake of carrying out marketing campaigns. It is upon you to observe the details, assimilate the points and then implement them to push your business to greater heights.

Use this book as the ultimate guide which in turn will push your business to higher rates of success. I hope you will be able to make the most out of this book and really have an effectively successful marketing campaign.

So, explore the different points and then be all set to enjoy the merits which this book has to offer. Automate the marketing efforts, put in the right budget and watch the results unfold right in front of you.

I will be more than happy to learn how this book has helped you in some way. If you feel you have learned something or you think it offered you some value, please take a moment to leave an honest review on Amazon. It would help many future readers who will be forever grateful to you. As I will!

To Your Success,
Adam Richards

DISCLAIMER AND/OR LEGAL NOTICES:

Every effort has been made to accurately represent this book and it's potential. Results vary with every individual, and your results may or may not be different from those depicted. No promises, guarantees or warranties, whether stated or implied, have been made that you will produce any specific result from this book. Your efforts are individual and unique, and may vary from those shown. Your success depends on your efforts, background and motivation.

The material in this publication is provided for educational and informational purposes. Use of the programs, advice, and information contained in this book is at the sole choice and risk of the reader.

www.ingramcontent.com/pod-product-compliance
Lightning Source LLC
Chambersburg PA
CBHW071233220526
45468CB00002B/838

* 9 7 8 1 7 9 8 4 5 0 5 5 0 *